John Wesley
Powell

VOYAGE OF DISCOVERY
The Story Behind the Scenery ®

text
by
Dan Murphy

photography
by
Gary Ladd

DAN MURPHY, a retired National Park Service interpretive specialist, claims the way to know a historic journey is to follow it. A boatman, he's floated the rivers and guided trips to follow Powell's voyage. Dan also wrote the earlier book in this series: *Lewis and Clark: Voyage of Discovery.*

GARY LADD, a professional photographer for 15 years, traversed the various reaches of the Colorado and Green rivers to record Powell's route of exploration. Gary's photographs heighten our awareness of the vulnerability of the still unspoiled lands along the rivers.

Front cover: Toroweap Overlook in Grand Canyon. Inside front cover: Flaming Gorge (now a reservoir). Page 1: Inner Gorge and Granite Falls Rapids. Pages 4/5: Tollgate Rock on Green River in Wyoming.

Edited by Mary L. Van Camp. Book design by K. C. DenDooven.

Second Printing, 1992
POWELL, VOYAGE OF DISCOVERY: THE STORY BEHIND THE SCENERY. © 1991 KC PUBLICATIONS, INC.
LC 91-60044. ISBN 0-88714-059-9.

John Wesley Powell
VOYAGE OF DISCOVERY

It was an unlikely crew, especially for what faced them: A boy still in his teens, an out-of-work printer, a disgruntled Army sergeant, a man afraid of the law, and an Englishman seeking adventure, to name a few. It follows that such a crew would also have an unlikely leader to boss them—and, make no mistake, boss them he did—a one-armed, mostly self-taught schoolteacher from the prairies. Yet this little band was about to change the map of the western United States. They would, in fact, *make* the map, going where few had gone before and even fewer had returned.

They were actually better qualified than they seemed. Although lacking a formal education—not unusual before the Civil War—John Wesley Powell as a youth had fallen in with a remarkable man, George Crookham, who believed in learning first hand. He took young Wes tramping about through the Ohio woods with eyes open and brains at work, which suited the young explorer-to-be just fine.

Later, expanding his horizons but keeping the method, Powell took solitary boat journeys down the Ohio, Mississippi, and Illinois rivers, as well as long exploratory hikes. (On one across Michigan he met Emma, leading to a good marriage that would last a lifetime.) These journeys were not mere adventures—he studied landforms, plants, and animals, applying what he knew and deducing more, even becoming a respectable specialist on clams and other mollusks.

When the Civil War broke out Powell was a schoolteacher in Illinois. (Qualifications were lax. And he just may have been the best teacher any of us ever wished we had.) Powell enlisted in the Union Army early, studied fortifications, and earned the trust of a rising general named Ulysses S. Grant. In charge of some of the ditch-work construction at the siege of Vicksburg, between shellings Powell scoured the sides of the ditches for fossil mollusks to add to his collection. At Shiloh, bloody Shiloh, a miniball shattered his right arm. Barely recovered from the amputation, he grimly continued fighting for the rest of the war.

When peace broadened down over the battered land, Powell and ten thousand others—including the men who would join him on the great adventure, though he didn't know it yet—returned home to rebuild a changed nation. Energies developed but diverted during the war now were turned westward, symbolized by the rail-

"*Running a Rapid,*" *woodcut prepared for Powell's 1875 "Report on the Exploration of the Colorado River." In later works Powell retained this woodcut while replacing others with photos. To the public, such desperate moments were the essence of the voyage.*

roads even then crawling up the slope of the plains toward the Rocky Mountains. Powell went back to teaching in Illinois but could not resist the lure of the young West. The boy in the boat, now grown-up, organized summer "field trips" with students and friends. Diverted from the Black Hills by Indian uprisings, they explored the Colorado Rockies. True, they were amateurs, but the land was so new! Practically everything they measured or sketched or plucked and took home was new to science.

It was during these explorations that Powell had his great idea. South and west of Denver the maps still had a great blank area: the canyons of the Colorado River. Travelers had gone around them on all sides, and there had been scattered reports as far back as Spanish exploration days of the awesome gashes and strangely eroded desert landscapes, but still it was a great blank on the maps.

Returning to the East, Powell ordered boats built he thought would withstand the rumored rapids, whirlpools and falls. With frontier brashness he approached Congress

Early in the spring of 1869 a party was organized for the exploration of the canyons....We were to descend the Green to the Colorado, and the Colorado down to the foot of the Grand Canyon.

Powell, just before May 23, 1869.

for support for his "scientific expedition." They brushed him aside, but from his old friend Grant, now General of the Army and soon to be president, he received the promise of rations to be issued at western posts to him and his men.

His men. Some of them were better prepared than it appeared at first, because preparation for this kind of exploration does not come from a classroom. The most competent in wilderness ways was John Sumner, a Rocky Mountain guide and outfitter that Powell had used in his early trips, and whom he now hired for the river trip. Sumner picked up others: Oramel Howland, a printer on the *Rocky Mountain News* who loved wilderness, and with him came his brother Seneca; William Dunn, trapper and mule packer with black hair flowing down his back, "for he has a sublime contempt of shears and razors"; and Billy Rhodes, who often used the name Hawkins and had some unknown scrape with the law in his background. The Major—Powell carried the Civil War title the rest of his life—took his brother, Walter, strong and willing but still suffering mentally from a Confederate prison.

At Fort Bridger Powell met George Bradley, a New Englander who knew something about boats and wanted desperately out of the Army, which Powell arranged through General Grant in order to get him on the expedition. At the last minute, almost ready to launch, an English adventurer named Frank Goodman showed up and asked to go along. Surprisingly, the Major took him, though it would not turn out to be a good decision. A better last minute find was young Andy Hall, a chip floating on the frontier flood who had already been a mule driver and bullwhacker for five years. The experience of war and of the frontier had molded these men, and they would need it. The Colorado would be no picnic, and three would not survive the trip.

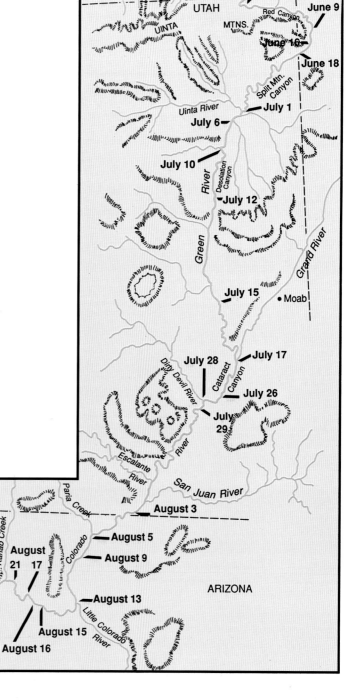

This was the blank space on the map that Powell and his men slowly, dangerously filled in. Dates here represent journal entries used in this book.

Who knows the intensity of a storm just over the horizon? Who could know these calm waters at "Tollgate Rock," Green River, Wyoming, led to thunderous rapids, beauty, hardship, and the career of one of America's great scientists?

The good people of Green River City, Wyoming, turn out to see us start. We raise our little flag, push the boats from shore, and the swift current carries us down....

The Colorado River system is like a capital "Y" with the arms, the Green and the Grand, coming together to form the Colorado proper. (Today the name "Grand" has been dropped, the old Grand and the Colorado together being today's Colorado.) Powell probably chose to start on the Green, at the little town of Green River, Wyoming, because the new railroad could deliver his boats there.

Today's river runners in safe, comfortable rafts may look with astonishment at Powell's cigar-shaped boats, almost guaranteed to roll in big water. But this was a new problem. Nobody had ever faced water such as awaited them now, and he worked with what he knew. Three of the boats were heavy oak, 21 feet long, with watertight compartments at either end. (Well, they seemed watertight when they built them, back on the Illinois prairies.) The boats were heavy, and when loaded with a ton of supplies each, would wallow like logs. The fourth boat, Powell's, was built of light pine, and only 16 feet long. The idea was that Powell would scout in the lighter boat and indicate the preferred route through big water by hand signals.

They packed the supplies into the boats at Green River: flour, coffee, and bacon; rifles, ammunition, and traps (part of the crew's pay was to be the opportunity to trap beaver along the way...which did not happen); tools, cooking gear, and bedding. Most important in Powell's eyes were the scientific instruments with which he would measure this unknown river and its canyons, bringing them from the mists of legend into reality, verified marks filling in the blank on the maps.

A mistake here, which they would realize later, was putting all the barometers into one boat instead of distributing them in case a boat was lost.

The men had named the boats but Powell assigned the crews. The Major's brother, Walter, and ex-sergeant George Bradley (he'd been out of the Army eight days now, and was probably still rejoicing) rowed the *Maid of the Cañon*. Billy Rhodes and young Andy Hall rowed *Kitty Clyde's Sister*—one suspects it was a lively boat—and the brothers Oramel and Seneca Howland were in the *No Name* with the Englishman, Frank Goodman. The Major had chosen Jack Sumner and Bill Dunn to row the pilot boat, the *Emma Dean,* while he would stand or sit in the bow and "read the water," the skill all boatmen have had to develop since.

They pushed off at 1:00 p.m., on the "high" you'd expect of such a moment. The river was kind to them at the beginning, which is a good thing as they had a lot to learn. Almost immediately young Andy Hall and Billy Rhodes in the *Kitty Clyde's Sister* ran aground on a sandbar, then pushed off only to run aground on the bank; Sumner got a kick out of the fledgling boatmen yelling "Gee" and "Haw" as the boat did what it wanted to in the Green's current. They camped just a couple of hours downstream. There was much to learn, but they were started.

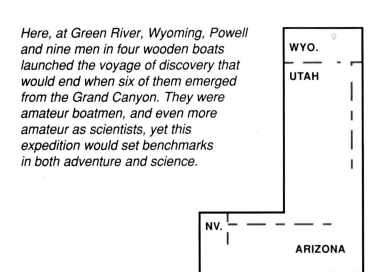

Here, at Green River, Wyoming, Powell and nine men in four wooden boats launched the voyage of discovery that would end when six of them emerged from the Grand Canyon. They were amateur boatmen, and even more amateur as scientists, yet this expedition would set benchmarks in both adventure and science.

Powell already knew the West better than most, from two land expeditions in the Rocky Mountains. Now he would learn the rivers.

*Today it rains, and we employ the time in repairing one of our barometers....
A new tube has to be put in; that is, a long glass tube has to be filled with mercury
four or five inches at a time, and each installment boiled over a spirit lamp. It is a
delicate task to do this without breaking the glass; but we have success, and are
ready to measure mountains once more.*

Rain. It was one thing to jump out of the boat into knee-deep water and push off, even to "take a bath" as Billy Rhodes did in a minor mishap, the kind that later would not even be noticed. But rain changes everything on the river, even the sound as it tattoos the water and whatever head covering they could scrounge to wear. They took their time in camp—"a leisurely breakfast," the record says—and near the mouth of Henry's Fork stopped to dig up a cache of supplies that the Major had packed in the previous spring. He was relieved to find the cache undisturbed, and idly wondered what Indians would have done with the chronometers, barometers, and sextant had they found them.

The Major knew what he would do with them. He was determined that this was a scientific expedition, not a river-running lark. Chronometer and sextant together would yield their position on the earth, and carefully drawn lines would begin to edge into the great blank on the maps. The barometers would tell them how high the cliffs were. They also told the explorers how much the river had descended, which also implied how much was left to descend before the river came out at the other side of the blank. Later this information of how much descent was left would move from marks on the map to the gut wrenching realization of how many rapids were left and how bad they were—but by then they would have no barometers.

For now, the trip was young and still an adventure, in spite of the continuous rain. The Major stayed for two days at a pleasant camp just before the river began to carve its way through the Uinta Mountains. Already they could see the brilliant reds of the gorge ahead, and even before they entered it they named it "Flaming Gorge." The men began to get into the "geologizing" the Major seemed so excited about. One wonders how the hickory-hewn outdoorsmen, hardened by war and wilderness, regarded this curious man. He was as tough as they were, yet seemed fascinated by the oddest things: the color of a rock, the precise sequence of strata, whether a layer continued at the same thickness or not. And these things were measured, not merely observed. When Bradley climbed the rising cliffs and scrambled over to look down into the gorge, they knew that he was 1,200 feet up. Climbs like this would become routine, as would the frustrations. On this one he could not find a way down into the gorge, and had to retreat to camp against a hard driving rain.

As the river cut into the Uinta Mountains it revealed the striking red layer that led the expedition to give the gorge this perfect name— "Flaming Gorge." To Powell, such strata were more than decoration, they were windows on the geologic past, and the men soon learned that stops meant climbing and measuring.

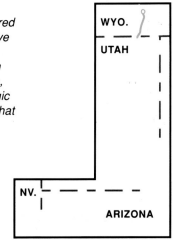

It was spring, and spring as well in the exploration of the West. Eastern eyes marveled at new plants, new vistas, new adventures, and new ideas.

...here we have our first experience with canyon rapids....we thread the narrow passage with exhilarating velocity, mounting the high waves, whose foaming crests dash over us, and plunging into the troughs, until we reach the quiet water below; and then comes a feeling of great relief....

Having practiced on kinder waters, they entered the gorge and for the first time encountered canyon rapids. Rapids which later they would class as mild or even ignore, now made them shout. River runners today recognize the feeling: the noise ahead, nervously standing to try to see what is coming. They soon realized this is often impossible, as you are looking over the lip of the rapid from above, and sometimes see only the line of water disappearing. Looking back you can see the froth and foam, but by then you are through it. Irresistibly the boat gathers speed, and now comes the ride. The exhilaration, if not the speed, can be measured by Oramel Howland's claim that they achieved the speed of a railroad train, "sixty miles an hour." They didn't, but the fledgling boatmen's heart rates did.

Those were the "good" rapids. Not all were so benign, and now they learned about "lining." When the Major, ahead in the *Emma Dean,* judged a rapid too dangerous to run he signaled the other boats to pull ashore. Then all hands turned-to, handling one boat at a time. Uncoiling ropes, they tied one to each end of the boat. Scrambling along the shore, sometimes in water up to their armpits and other times climbing over rocks, straining mightily on the ropes, they let the boat pass down unmanned, using the ropes and current to guide it around rocks.

At the worst rapid so far they had to unload the cargo as well, lugging it 200 yards around the rapid and then lining the lightened boats through, then reloading. This was close to three tons of cargo, every leaden pound of it lifted once to get it out of the boats, staggered around the rapids, and lifted again back into the boats.

During the portage they encountered history when someone noticed faded letters scratched on a rock: "Ashley 1835." (Actually it was 1825.) They didn't know the story, but this was as far as fur trader William Ashley had gotten a half-century before, spinning down the Green in a "bullboat" shaped like a cereal bowl. Now that must have been a ride!

Already known to trappers, Brown's Park was a respite from the increasing rapids. There was even a "natural show," as the men were entertained by the aerobatics and songs of countless swallows.

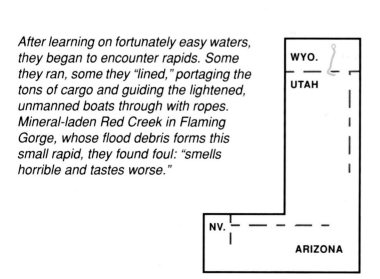

After learning on fortunately easy waters, they began to encounter rapids. Some they ran, some they "lined," portaging the tons of cargo and guiding the lightened, unmanned boats through with ropes. Mineral-laden Red Creek in Flaming Gorge, whose flood debris forms this small rapid, they found foul: "smells horrible and tastes worse."

WYO.

UTAH

NV.

ARIZONA

...See the boat strike a rock...careen and fill the open compartment with water. Two of the men lose their oars; she swings around, and is carried down at a rapid rate, broadside on, for a few yards, and strikes amidships on another rock with great force, is broken quite in two, and the men are thrown into the river; the larger part of the boat floating buoyantly, they soon seize it, and down the river they drift, past the rocks for a few hundred yards to a second rapid, filled with huge boulders, where the boat strikes again, and is dashed to pieces, and the men and fragments are soon carried beyond my sight. Running along I turn a bend, and see a man's head above the water, washed about in a whirlpool below a great rock....

Now it was rapid after rapid, and they named the canyon "Lodore" remembering the cascades in the Robert Southey poem: "Advancing and prancing and glancing and dancing, Recoiling, turmoiling, and toiling, and boiling..." (It was young Andy Hall, bullwhacker since he was 13, who remembered the lines. The frontier produced strange combinations.) And here they met disaster.

Powell saw a rapid too dangerous to run, pulled ashore and signaled the other boats to follow. Two did, but the *No Name,* perhaps still bailing from a riffle shortly before, missed the landing and helplessly surged into the rapid. Haystacks of water and rocks tore the oars from the boatmen. Thrown overboard (it's not uncommon to be thrown out of a boat without the boat itself tipping), the men scrambled to hold on to the careening craft but in seconds it hit a huge boulder and smashed in two.

The frantic watchers saw wreckage, and heads like small black balls floating in the roller-coaster waves. The danger was not over. Oramel and Seneca Howland got to an island, which scarcely improved their situation, but Goodman was worse, clinging for life to a slippery boulder midstream. With a pole they pulled him to the island, and reliable Jack Sumner showed the boatmanship he'd developed by rescuing them with the lighter *Emma Dean.*

It was a somber night, even with all hands temporarily safe. The first major rapid and a boat was gone, with a third of the provisions. Worse, all of the barometers had been on that boat by mistake. But the river gods relented. The next morning they found half the boat stuck on a rock and, with what the Major thought was commendable enthusiasm, Sumner and Hall got to the wreck and found the barometers. But it turned out the enthusiasm was over a jug of whiskey they'd smuggled on at Green River. It was good medicine, and they were ready for it.

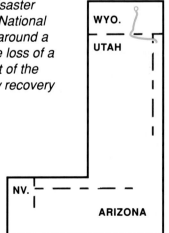

The "No Name" swamped in Disaster Falls (in present-day Dinosaur National Monument), then broke in two around a rock. The crew escaped but the loss of a ton of supplies affected the rest of the expedition—even with the lucky recovery of a jug of illicit whiskey.

WYO.

UTAH

NV.

ARIZONA

As bad as the river was, the men saw battered debris left by even higher, more violent water. Each rise was a worry—how high would it go?

...a whirlwind comes, scattering the fire among the dead willows and cedar-spray, and seen there is a conflagration. The men rush for the boats...their clothing burned and hair singed....Just below is a rapid, filled with rocks. On they shoot, no channel explored, no signal to guide them....

In Lodore Canyon the men began to realize what the river had in store for them, and the river began to measure the men too. Rapid after rapid, until Bradley concluded it was just one long rapid. Running was dangerous, portaging was backbreaking. A rock stove in the side of the *Kitty Clyde's Sister*, which meant repair and climbing out of the canyon to find pitch for patching. The journals record a few injuries—Bradley received a bad gash over his eye along here—but by now cuts and bruises were common. Rocks are sharp and unforgiving. While being lined the *Maid of the Cañon* swamped, yanking the rope from the five men holding it and burning their water-softened hands. It shot free through the rapid but for once fortune smiled on them. Frantically scrambling downstream they found the boat turning safely in an eddy.

Nor was camp much relief. Clothing and bedding and supplies were soaked, and even when dried would not stay that way long in the wild water. The Howland brothers and Goodman, crew of the *No Name*, were without personal gear and spare clothes, wet or dry, after the wreck. Rest had to come where you were when night fell, not at some carefully chosen campsite. Bradley recorded, "If I had a dog that would lie where my bed is made tonight I would kill him and burn his collar and swear I never owned him."

Troubles were not only in the water. Hunting and fishing failed, and they were digging into their already-depleted supplies deeper than the Major liked. Then came the fire, insult after injury. A sudden whirlwind,

still a bane of river runners, scattered their cookfire into the tinder-dry brush covering the narrow area of the bench they were camped on, instantly setting it aflame. The Major, watching helplessly from the cliff above, saw the men rush for the boats, their only retreat.

One man stumbled and the cooking gear he was carrying disappeared into the brown waters; they would make an art of jury-rigging after this. They cut loose and had to run the rapid that waited, unscouted. With singed hair, in wet bedding, hands torn and bruised, they were learning that the river had surprises for them. But what were the choices? Sleep fitfully, get up to coffee and biscuits, and lug another hundred pounds over the rocky shoreline. Downstream was the only way out.

The river was taking its toll, in battered boats and bruised men. Even camp was not a sure relief, as when a whirlwind spread their campfire through the brush. They escaped with singed hair and beards, and only minor loss of gear, but it was a lesson in caution—as if they needed it!

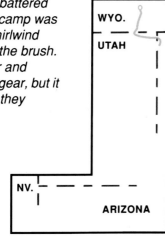

The plan had been to supplement their supplies by hunting, and when they shot an occasional bighorn sheep or deer it was a godsend. More often they settled for beans and coffee.

*...I gain a foothold in a little crevice, and grasp an angle of the rock overhead.
I find I can get up no farther, and cannot step back....Standing on my toes,
my muscles begin to tremble. It is sixty or eighty feet to the foot of the precipice.
If I lose my hold I shall fall to the bottom, and then perhaps roll over the bench....
At this instant it occurs to Bradley to take off his drawers, which he does, and
swings them down to me. I hug close to the rock, let go with my hand, seize the
dangling legs and, with his assistance, I am enabled to gain the top....*

Relief came suddenly, as the river finished its mad attack on the Uinta Range. For ten days they had been toiling through the gash where the river carved the pediment of the range, with a roar that echoed day and night. Now the canyon walls lowered, the country flattened out, and the Yampa came flowing in from the east. They called the cliff across from the mouth of the Yampa "Echo Rock" and played like boys, yelling across to it. Here they stayed in camp two days, drying gear and repairing it, redeeming what they could of the constantly soaked flour. They tried their best while memories were fresh to duplicate the map Howland had been keeping on the *No Name,* lost in the wreck.

Perhaps it came with too many hours in the boats, but they did hike! Climbing out on the west side of the river they were astonished to cross a narrow rock and look down at the river again, and realized they were camped at the beginning of a huge gooseneck. Other climbs were prodigious. Billy Rhodes managed to shoot a big deer up on top, and he and Goodman brought in what they could carry, leaving one forequarter hanging from a tree. The next day Bradley, who had heard about it in camp, decided to go get the forequarter. In his journal it seems a matter of course that he hiked out, *found* it, and noted by the barometer he'd carried along that he was 2,800 feet above the river. (That's like climbing the stairs of the Empire State Building three times in a row.) Then he carried the forequarter back to camp.

The next few days, during which Powell apparently was saved by Bradley's "drawers," were classic river running. There were challenging rapids but short of terrifying, and scenery you can visit today; they were floating through what would one day be Dinosaur National Monument. Trout for breakfast, mosquitoes at night, and finally they came to the mouth of the Uinta River, a place they had been waiting for.

Explorers-though they were, they were not the first people in the canyon country by a millennium, as documented by these Indian petroglyphs. Powell's omnivorous interests included Indians as well as geology, both on the journey and for the rest of his life.

Relief from rapids came with a price, rowing the heavy wooden boats in the June heat. They slowly moved through a geological wonderland, Powell looking and thinking. He did find fossils here, though not the remarkable dinosaur quarry discovered much later and set aside as Dinosaur National Monument.

WYO.

UTAH

NV.

ARIZONA

...*This morning, with two of the men, I start for the [Uinta] agency. It is a toilsome walk, twenty miles of the distance being across a sand desert....*

This was their last brush with civilization before plunging into the blank space on the map; there could be no turning back, nor even contact, after this. Thirty miles up the Uinta River was the Ute Indian Agency, and Powell had made arrangements to have mail delivered to them there. Maybe they would even be able to replace the supplies that had been lost in the wreck of the *No Name*. They camped a few days at the mouth of the river, finishing maps and letters to be carried out.

Andy Hall and Walter Powell hiked out first, then the Major hiked out with Billy Rhodes and the Englishman, Frank Goodman. It was the last they would see of Goodman. He'd lost all his personal gear in the boat wreck (as had the Howland brothers) and, having lost his taste for adventuring, he left the expedition here.

Back at the river camp the men left behind waited. The mosquitoes were awful (Bradley even recorded a conversation with one), but there were currants, good fishing, and they shot geese, though they were lean in the summer heat. Bradley made beans—and did he make beans! Apparently not a cook, he had no idea how they'd swell and ended up with twelve quarts, he estimated. They passed the Fourth of July there, and talked of where they'd been on other Fourths. How one would like to have stood just outside the firelight to hear their Civil War talk. Once before when their guns had echoed off the cliffs and sent sheep running, one man remarked on other days, when they'd "made the cliffs ring, while others did the scampering!"

The Major enjoyed his visit to the Ute agency with his usual voracious intellectual curiosity. He noted the agricultural development in the Uinta Valley, and his journal begins to talk about the role of irrigation in the West, a subject that would occupy him much of his life. (One wonders if he had any inkling then that one day he would be a partner in a ranch in this very valley.) But more immediate problems pressed. Powell sent back two Ute packers, but what they were bringing was disappointing. He had been able to obtain only 300 pounds of flour, slim pickings to replace the entire cargo of the *No Name*.

They repacked the gear and set up new crews, with Seneca Howland joining Bradley and Walter Powell on the *Maid of the Cañon*, while his brother joined the *Kitty Clyde's Sister* crew of Billy Rhodes and Andy Hall. It was time to go on, to where the Indians had told the Major the river disappeared underground and from which no one could emerge. For three of the men now coiling the ropes and wading through the mud to push off the boats, the Indians were right.

Those who waited for the resupply party fished and hunted, with medium success. Their journal entries express impatience to be on their way again.

Battered, one boat down, they felt like veterans as they finished the first phase of the journey. At the Uinta River they hiked 30 miles to an Indian agency for their last chance for supplies, and found little. One man quit, and the rest pushed off into unknown waters.

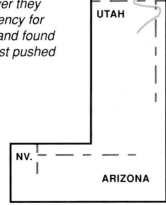

WYO.

UTAH

NV.

ARIZONA

"Potato tops are not good greens on the sixth day of July."

The expedition could have come to an anticlimactic end the day they left the mouth of the Uinta. On the sandbar formed where the White River comes in from the east they found an untended garden. The potatoes were not near ready but they helped themselves to the greens, which young Andy Hall assured them were "good eating." They aren't, and soon the hardy members of the exploration party were rolling on the ground, retching. They recovered in an hour or so, but it was a frightening time. It doesn't take a mountain to kill a man.

Jack Sumner wrote a curious statement in his journal about this incident, and it may have some bearing on the question of Major Powell's relationship with the men, a subject of controversy in later years. The Major usually ruled with an iron fist, and has been criticized for it. But the roles may have been familiar ones. Powell had been an officer in the Union Army, the other men were enlisted. Now it was a dangerous expedition and he was in charge. One doubts that modern "group supervision" methods would have cut much weight with this group of frontiersmen!

But beyond this they really seem to have enjoyed his science, at least before their situation became desperate. Recognizing terrain that looked like that up around Fort Bridger, they were pleased when the Major showed with fossils that it was of the same formation. They learned to use the scientific instruments he'd brought along. And this was still Powell the teacher, on the grandest field trip of his life.

The statement Sumner makes is, "Potato tops are not good greens on the sixth day of July." It's an odd statement, but demonstrates classic scientific caution in not going beyond the data! One imagines Powell and the intelligent, practical frontiersman Sumner during the long days and hours when the current was slow, the rowing steady, the conversation comfortable and rambling. Powell would not have passed a chance with captive students such as this. They likely knew as much as they cared to know about what he observed in the strata and formations they passed. Here was scientific method, nothing assumed: "Potato tops are not good greens *on the sixth day of July.*"

Now they entered a gray, heat-blasted canyon, seemingly devoid of life. They named it "Desolation Canyon" but had to admit that the scenery was overwhelming, and not just from the river. When they climbed to the rim they saw goblins and ships, a landscape of eroded fantasy stretching on both sides of the canyon's cut through it. This scenery was strikingly different from anything they'd seen before.

Receding high water often leaves marshes along calmer stretches of the river, where the explorers hunted geese and fished. Unfortunately, the marshes produce more mosquitoes than anything else!

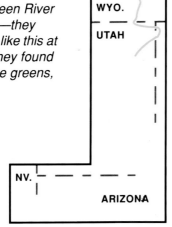

Ever the boatman's friend, the cottonwood trees along the Green River provided shade, boat ties, fuel—they meant "camp." On a sandbank like this at the mouth of the White River they found young potato plants and ate the greens, with near disastrous results.

...Howland and myself determine to climb out, and start up a lateral canyon, taking a barometer with us, for the purpose of measuring the thickness of the strata over which we pass....

Major Powell chose a curious way of measuring the thickness of the strata along the river. It may have been one of the gaps in his self-taught education, as better ways were available and he'd use them later in his career. Now, he and whoever was to help that day would match chronometers and barometers, with someone assigned to stay below. Then they'd climb the cliff, and at half-hour intervals both they and the people in camp would record the barometric pressure.

Thus, though they'd long lost touch with "true" barometric pressure, relative pressure would tell them the altitude difference between the barometers. This means, of course, that if the layer they were ascending was easy or thin, they'd be there early, and explore until time to take the reading. On the other hand, thick layers or inaccessible ones would force them to climb frantically, or risk having to wait for the next half-hourly reading.

Climbing with barometers was no picnic, especially once they were in a "chimney," a vertical crack somewhat thicker than a man's body. The trick was to wedge your back on one wall and your knees and hands or elbows on the other, and work your way up. Carrying clumsy wooden instruments, of course, made it harder. Powell, in the lead, would wedge himself, and hold the instruments while his companion passed him in the crack. Then Powell handed him the instruments and made his way up beyond him, to repeat the process. Not a bad trick for a one-armed man.

The pilot boat, the *Emma Dean*, rolled. She had broken two oars and was pulling with only two, while the crew looked for timber suitable to fashion replacements, when a reflex wave filled her and another rolled her. Powell was thrown out but floated easily in his cork life jacket, the only one on the trip. Finally the river flushed them into quieter water. As they struggled ashore Powell retrieved a blanket roll that was floating by. One doubts that his one-armed condition was talked about much.

In some places deeper than the Grand Canyon, Desolation Canyon was almost treeless, and spotted with rapids. The sense of cutting into the earth was inescapable.

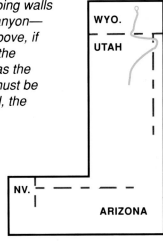

The Major's insistence on climbing walls such as these in Desolation Canyon— and often the mountains just above, if there were any—often slowed the expedition, but in his mind it was the reason for the trip. The rocks must be examined, the strata measured, the river's twisting course charted.

WYO.

UTAH

NV.

ARIZONA

...Bradley is knocked over the side, but his foot catching under the seat, he is dragged along in the water, with his head down: making great exhertion, he seizes the gunwale with his left hand, and can lift his head above the water now and then...

Yet another way a river can kill a man, even while he's holding onto the boat. While Bradley was dragged along they were rapidly sweeping toward an over-hung cliff; big, moody Walter Powell pulled mightily on the oars to avoid scraping Bradley off on the cliff, then pulled him in. Adventures like this were becoming so routine, they hardly seemed worthy of mention by the weary men.

In another place they met a situation that demanded a new way of lining. The river filled the canyon wall to wall, with no passage on either side; yet here was a rock-choked rapid that must be lined. Snubbing the line they let one man and boat down to a rock, as far as they could; and while holding that one, let another down to him. He fastened the second line to his own boat and let the newcomer down, now two lines distant from the beginning. Repeating the process got the boats through, but left a man (Dunn) up on the rock. Holding onto the line he jumped in and swam, being pulled out by his companions below. Hardly worth mentioning. Actually they thought it was a blessing, given the alternative of lugging the gear along a makeshift trail.

A culture note, post-Civil War. Andy Hall was singing "with a voice like a crosscut saw" a tune that Bradley doubted would "rank with America and other national anthems." He copied the words to the chorus of the new song:

> *When he put his arm around her,*
> *She bustified like a forty pounder,*
> *Look away, look away, look away, Dixie Land.*

Desolation Canyon earned its name, with blasting desert winds that sandpapered them in the day, and piled sand under the blankets and tarps at night. Finally they left it, reentered what they called Coal Canyon, and had the exhilaration a boatman craves: fast water, few rocks, a free ride. It flattened into another valley and they briefly touched history again: Gunnison Crossing, and before that the ford on the Old Spanish Trail to California, where today lies the town of Green River, Utah, and the crossing of an interstate and a railroad. Places to cross the river are rare in canyon country, and you must take them where you find them.

They labored through Desolation and Gray canyons in baking heat, the silent afternoons an oven. Rare streams such as Rock Creek were jewels of relief but could be enjoyed only briefly. The men knew they were just a third of the way at best.

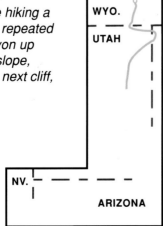

Climbing walls such as these in Desolation Canyon was not like hiking a modern park service trail. It was repeated effort: Find a crack or side canyon up the cliff, scramble up the talus slope, search for another crack up the next cliff, then another talus slope.

WYO.

UTAH

NV.

ARIZONA

*...There is an exquisite charm in our ride today down this beautiful canyon.
It gradually grows deeper with every mile of travel; the walls are symmetrically
curved, and grandly arched; of a beautiful color, and reflected
in the quiet waters in many places....*

After the Gunnison Valley came days in Labyrinth Canyon, then Stillwater Canyon. These are favorite calm-water-boating canyons today, and apparently the Major thought so too, to judge by the quote above. But tiredness, hunger, perhaps even worry were wearing on the men, and here they had to row steadily. Bradley wrote in the same stretch: "...we float along on a muddy stream walled in by huge sandstone bluffs that echo back the slightest sound. Hardly a bird save the ill-omened raven or an occasional eagle screaming over us; one feels a sense of loneliness as he looks on the little party, only three boats and nine men, hundreds of miles from civilization..."

They passed tufa terraces laid down by mineral-laden waters from a spring they judged extinct. It may have been, but in recent years energy prospectors sunk a pipe into it and now it occasionally gushes like a geyser. The canyon walls began to rise, not back to the awesome heights of Desolation Canyon but well over 300 feet, and these were red sandstone. It was hot and that wore on the spirit, but the cliffs were spectacular in early and late light, and reflected in the water.

The river coiled and wound like a snake, a river that once had crawled lazily across a plain in oxbows, but now the same shape lay entrenched 300 feet in the red rock. They passed Trin-Alcove bend, one of the wonderful spots in this stretch, where three exquisite side canyons come together with one mouth. They scrambled over a notch to find the river going the

other way on the other side, and called it "Bowknot Bend," the name it bears today.

"Sour beans" gave them problems one night; could these have been leftovers from Bradley's experiment back at the mouth of the Uinta? They ate a beaver, and a goose when lucky enough to bag one. These were slow, hot miles, even with the beauty. They should have enjoyed it. The river was letting them rest, but though they could not know it, it was about to earn its reputation.

The journals speak more of action on the river, but occasionally there are glimpses of life in camp, of horseplay, campfire conversations, and rest from the day.

After Desolation Canyon the river slowed and twisted lazily through Labyrinth Canyon, the walls lower but now spectacularly colored sandstone. The reflections must have been as enchanting as modern boatmen find them, but the journals speak more of the labor of rowing in the slow water.

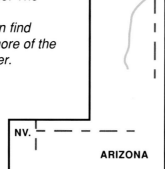

...An hour of this rapid running brings us to the junction of the Grand and the Green....These streams unite in solemn depths more than one thousand two hundred feet below the general surface of the country....

Before the Expedition had started, certain things were known about the Colorado River system. Imagine a capital "Y", but with a blot obscuring the junction. That was the "Unknown" on the map. It was known that the Grand started in the Rocky Mountains west of Denver and disappeared into the Unknown, and that the Green, the other upper arm, disappeared into it as well. But the only river that came out was the Colorado, known over in Nevada where it emerged from the Unknown and flowed on to the Gulf of California.

There was even a Mormon settlement near that emergence, Callville, a name that must have assumed the properties of "paradise" to the hungry men hoping to get there. Somewhere in that Unknown the Green and the Grand must join to form the Colorado, but no one knew where, not within a hundred miles.

They came upon it suddenly. Leaving Stillwater Canyon the current had picked up for an hour, which sometimes signaled trouble, but suddenly a stream large as the Green came in from the left. It had to be the Grand. Instantly dissipated was the fog of previous claims of a Colorado mountebank that he had laid out a city at the junction. The critical spot was trapped in the earth, shadowed by cliffs over 1,200 feet high, with barely enough room to camp at the junction of the three canyons.

It was important to fix the position of this junction carefully, and the Major decided to stay until August 7, when a solar eclipse would give him precise time (and therefore positioning) data. But his plans changed. The equipment and food situation was becoming critical. Their flour had been wetted repeatedly; when they

sieved what was left through mosquito netting they had to discard 200 pounds.

Of course they climbed, and years later Powell expended some of his most expressive prose describing the eroded, cut, phantasmagorical land they saw. (With reasonable effort you can see it today; it is Canyonlands National Park. And it still defies description.) Still, as important and as beautiful as this spot was, they had to leave. Supplies were low, and there was no replenishing here. On July 21 they left, and four miles downstream all hell broke loose!

The Confluence was critically important to geography as well as to their journey. They climbed out to fix its position, and were startled by the fantasy of landforms Canyonlands National Park visitors see today in the Needles District.

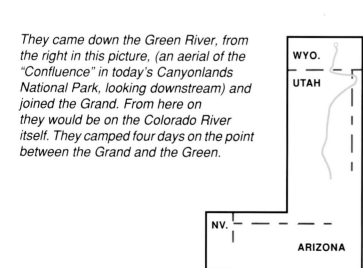

They came down the Green River, from the right in this picture, (an aerial of the "Confluence" in today's Canyonlands National Park, looking downstream) and joined the Grand. From here on they would be on the Colorado River itself. They camped four days on the point between the Grand and the Green.

WYO.

UTAH

NV.

ARIZONA

*...as fast as I can run...and tell the men there is a river coming down the canyon.
We carry our camp equipage hastily from the bank....Then we stand by,
and see the river roll on to join the Colorado....*

Just an hour onto the Colorado itself, still rowing through morning shade reflecting the towering cliffs, and the boat in front began to hear low thunder. The Colorado was about to earn its name. Two frightening days later they would name this "Cataract Canyon." Today, even semi-tamed with modern equipment, "Cat" is a boatman's favorite, one of the great stretches of virtually continuous rapids in the country. But these men, on their virgin trip as boatmen, on the edge of starvation with no chance of supply and no way back, floated into Cataract Canyon with no idea what was ahead, imprisoned in leading wooden boats shaped like cigars.

In Cataract Canyon the left bank is part of a landmass that is sliding (geologic time scale, like fingernails growing) toward the river. The continual supply of broken rock forms the rapids. The Major noticed the peculiar set of geological tilts this produces, and hit on something surprisingly close to the right answer. But for the men, the rapids were work pure and simple, heavy labor while the canyon baked at over 100 degrees.

The Major was cautious—losing that flour at the Confluence weighed on him—and they lined virtually everything. In one stretch the rapids came a hundred yards apart. It was pack, lift, stagger, reload. At the worst rapids, even the ponderous boats had to be skidded around. The men cleared paths as best they could in places where even walking was scrambling, and then pushed, heaved and pulled, dwarfed in the din of the rapid beside them.

The *Emma Dean* swamped and lost three oars. They stopped to carve some from cottonwood driftwood and repair the boats. The Major and two men started up a side canyon to fetch pitch from trees 1,500 feet up on the rim. Only the Major found a route up, collected two pounds of pitch in his empty sleeve, and started down. A typical afternoon storm seemed refreshing until he realized a flash flood was gathering in the side canyon leading to camp. He ran down the canyon ahead of the flash, warned the men and they moved the gear in time to watch the muddy waters go by. Just how many more surprises did this river have?

A great river should have a dramatic beginning. The rolling Colorado is, in fact, the culmination of the storms that dot the American West any summer afternoon, and the winter's quiet snowfall.

The Colorado is the daughter, not the mother, of her tributaries. When the sky turns leaden and it rains anywhere on the plateau, the waters can gather in even a small side canyon and race toward the river. Powell successfully raced one such flash flood back to camp.

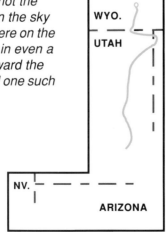

WYO.

UTAH

NV.

ARIZONA

Overleaf: *Sunset in Desolation Canyon. Occasionally the day's labor and danger brought such a blessing as this.*

*...After supper we sit by our campfire,
made of driftwood caught by the rocks,
and tell stories of wildlife; for the men
have seen such in the mountains or on the
plains....It is late before we spread
our blankets on the beach.*

...We discover the mouth of a stream, which enters from the right...it is "a dirty devil," and by this name the river is to be known hereafter. The water is exceedingly muddy, and has an unpleasant odor....

Cataract Canyon continued its assault on the expedition's food supplies, boats, bodies, and morale. Grumbling appears in the diaries. The *Emma Dean* caught in a whirlpool and spun, but came out with only one oar lost. It was another part of the cumulative lesson the river was teaching.

On a red-letter day they shot two mountain sheep, and feasted. Food in the stomach, cheer in the journals: "Two fine young sheep? We care not for bread or beans or dried apples tonight; coffee and mutton are all we ask." After supper Billy Rhodes wandered down by the boats and got out the sextant, "a strange proceeding for him" the Major wrote. When asked about it Billy said he was "trying to find the latitude and longitude of the nearest pie."

They found a fresh moccasin track and wondered about it, but were not too surprised. There were Indians in the canyon country, and how many tracks did they miss as they floated by?

Sitting around in camp after supper, they checked and reworked the approximate altitude readings their barometers gave them. How much vertical descent was left until the end? These rapids were worse than anything before. Could they be sure the "fall" continued in little pieces, bad as these were? Or somewhere were they going to find a log of the distance they had to descend, in one impossible falls?

The journals mention Andy Hall down by the river throwing stones across it, while Powell sat and stared at it, sometimes an hour at a time. "Darkness is coming on, but the waves are rolling with crests of foam so white they seem almost to give a light of their own....Where there are sunken rocks the water heaps up in mounds...and on the river tumbles and rolls." They knew this was not the worst the canyon could give them. They saw driftwood lodged in the rocks 60 feet up, sometimes they estimated 100 feet up. "God help the poor wretch that is caught in this canyon during high water," allowed Sumner.

But end this thundering canyon had to, and it did so about as suddenly as it had begun. As the walls lowered, a completely unexpected river came rolling in—well, trickling in—on the right. It stank, and they named it the "Dirty Devil," but it was significant. It was over three centuries since the Spaniard Vasquez de Coronado had come to the Rio Grande, over two centuries since the voyage of Marquette and Joliet on the Mississippi, and now these frontiersmen led by the one-armed schoolteacher had just discovered and named (for Europeans, at least) the last unknown river in the United States. And the mountain range this last-discovered river skirted to come to the Colorado? Today they are called the Henry Mountains, the last range in the country to be discovered and named, also by Powell. They were, in fact, filling in the map.

Today, Lake Powell backs well into the Dirty Devil Canyon, with modern powerboaters passing hundreds of feet above the 1869 campsites.

The "Dirty Devil" was a completely unexpected river, the last major U.S. river to be discovered. The expedition, by its constant climbing and careful map making, gained a sense of the Colorado as part of a wide drainage, something often missed by modern river runners trapped in the narrow main canyon.

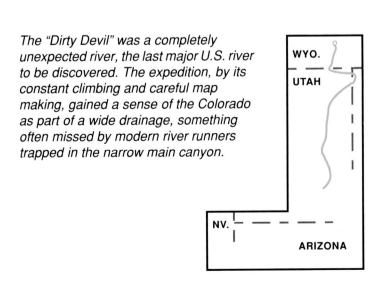

...Here I stand, where these now lost people stood centuries ago, and look over this strange country. I gaze off to great mountains...slowly covered by the night...and then I return to camp. It is no easy task to find my way down the wall in the darkness, and I clamber about until it is nearly midnight, before I arrive.

The river gave them a reprieve after the chaos of Cataract Canyon. For one stretch the gift was almost *too* good—it was nerve wracking. The river straightened to a race through a chute, and the cliff walls came straight into the water on both sides. It was a free ride at exhilarating speed, but what if an unrunnable rapid came now? It didn't, they flushed through and probably wished they could do it again, this time knowing they'd make it. But upstream thoughts are futile on the river.

They began to find Indian ruins, and stopped to examine them even with the press of their dwindling supplies. There were overhangs with smoke-blackened roofs, and debris on the floor. Where the canyon widened enough to have once held fields, they found the ruins of a dwelling on top of a bluff, and smaller structures, almost certainly for grain storage, on ledges in the cliff face. The dwelling showed remains of a second story and Powell guessed it may have had a third. Petroglyphs covered the cliffs near the ruins—Powell called them "etchings." Trying to climb out of the canyon for more observations, Powell found himself using Anasazi-carved steps and even a rickety prehistoric ladder.

Further downstream they found another ruin, a surface dwelling on a bluff. Here Powell instantly made a connection, recognizing that a below-ground structure in the ruins was the same "kiva," or ceremonial chamber, he's seen at living villages in the Hopi country. The term had not been adopted yet but he was looking at "Anasazi" ruins, and the great "mystery" of where the Anasazi had gone was no mystery to him. Today's Pueblo people, and Powell would get to know them well, are the Anasazi, descended to us to live amongst pickup trucks and TV antennas.

Powell also recognized another problem that still starts debates in archaeological circles. Why did the Anasazi sometimes choose to live in cliffs, difficult of access? In the days before specialization built its walls, Powell was geologist or anthropologist, depending on what new wonder the canyon had just revealed to him. Somewhere—one wishes to know where, but we don't—Powell had the vision that he would bring into reality as the Bureau of American Ethnography, and he would be its first director. Stopping to look at the ruins was not wasted time.

Powell and his men explored ruins whenever they found them, such as this prehistoric dwelling in Gypsum Canyon, often wondering how people had lived in this rugged terrain. Later Powell would spend as much time on these questions as on geological ones.

Powell was learning to read the story behind the rocks like a book, and we know from scattered comments in the journals that the men occasionally did so too. Here, obviously, had once been a beach, its fossil ripple marks now frozen in desert sandstone.

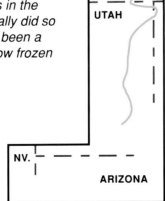

WYO.

UTAH

NV.

ARIZONA

...We have a curious ensemble of wonderful features—carved walls, royal arches, glens, alcove gulches, mounds, and monuments. From which of these features shall we select a name? We decide to call it Glen Canyon....

Erosion is an artist and a miracle. The forces seem random, almost chaotic, with water running this way and that as it wishes. The rocks the water and wind hit are likewise random, some sandstone, some limestone, some the hard basalts brought from deep in the molten earth. Yet the process is not random, and somehow it produces beauty. Water strikes a rock at a certain angle and velocity, and in geologic time that rock will assume a gentle curve reflecting the forces that worked on it, sometimes sweeping to a sharp edge.

As this happens to all rocks simultaneously, they become a garden of geometric delights. If sandstone collected as dunes before it solidified and hardened, the form of those dunes is in the rock, and erosion will reveal it. Textures, sweeps, repeated angles, all tell the story of what was there to begin with, and how erosion carved it.

They struggled with names for this canyon, called it "Mound Canyon," then "Monument Canyon," and finally the name it kept while it lived, "Glen Canyon." It had a thousand special places.

They had been looking for the San Juan River, which they knew had to come in from the east, some-where along here. It was not remarkable when it did, a stream "30 yards wide and 15 inches deep, dirty as well can be, but not as salty as most of the side streams are," coming in from a narrow canyon. They knew that for the maps they were drawing it was particularly important to carefully fix the position of the mouths of rivers, but the canyon around here made it difficult to make astronomical observations, so the Major moved camp downstream a mile.

There they found shade too, and it was welcome; their thermometers showed 104 degrees. But what scenery, even in the heat! They found an immense alcove almost 200 feet high, a narrow slot to the sky at the top, and Sumner thought it could contain 2,000 people. Some of the men carried what blankets and sleeping gear they had into it, and when Walter Powell burst into the old song "Old Shadey" and they heard the echo, they named it "Music Temple."

Nor was this the only wonder. They shot another sheep, ate what they could and dried more, winning a skirmish in the holding action with their dwindling supplies. The next day they ferried Powell across the river to where he could hike out and get a fix on the surrounding country, and they slept in Music Temple a second time. It may be the two days on the journey modern boatmen envy the most.

Glen Canyon was "the between place," rest and beauty for what they'd accomplished, a pause before the chaos to come.

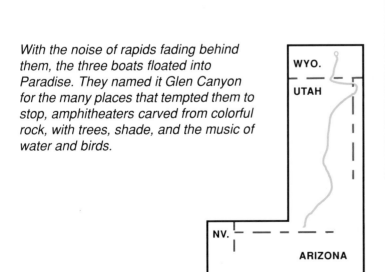

With the noise of rapids fading behind them, the three boats floated into Paradise. They named it Glen Canyon for the many places that tempted them to stop, amphitheaters carved from colorful rock, with trees, shade, and the music of water and birds.

WYO.

UTAH

NV.

ARIZONA

...We have learned to closely observe the texture of the rock. In softer strata, we have a quiet river; in harder, we find rapids and falls....

Recess in paradise was over, and the noise of rapids returned. Danger alerts the senses and makes a good teacher, even for non-geologists. The crew had learned to "read the rock" for what it might tell them about the rapids. Soft rock meant easy running, perhaps riffles but not the haystacks of water that meant hard portages in hard rock areas.

They also learned to notice the dip of the rock strata the river was carving through. If the rock layers dipped "away" from you, downstream, the river tended to run down the slope, often with great velocity but without many rapids. But, if the river looped and came the other way, which often it did, it now had to cut across the upturned ends of those same strata, with rapids and falls. Now, peering anxiously down the canyon, they saw the same limestones and hard sandstones they had seen in Cataract Canyon, and knew the rapids were back.

This was a hard time, the middle of the ordeal. They were too far from the end of the journey to yet have the "lift" of almost-done, and the work was hard, with little progress they could see. They encountered another stretch where the river surged through a chute with "freight train speed," with cliffs plunging straight into the water on either side, only this time they could see the spray of a rapid far down. It had to be scouted, but how?

They found they could pull their boats to the cliff on one side. One man stood in the boat and another man climbed up and stood on his shoulders, reaching a horizontal crevice in the cliff. Edging their way downstream, then standing as it became a shelf, they came to a place where the shelf had broken down and slid into the river. They edged their way back, collected driftwood and passed it along the crevice to the broken-down place, where they used it to fashion a "bridge" and went further...and still couldn't see the rapids well enough. So they came back, climbed up *out* of the canyon, looked from the rim and decided the rapid should not be run but could be lined.

But how to get to it? They repeated the technique they'd developed weeks ago, letting one boat down as far as its line would go and snubbing it. Then they let another down to the first boat, snubbed its line and let it on down another line's length, and finally had all three boats strung out. Then they re-collected at the bottom, near the head of the rapid where once again at least there were banks, even if just piled rocks. Then they lined the rapid.

It was all in a day's work, but these men were weary. Griping becomes constant in the journals of the men, some of it aimed at the Major for his insistence on stopping for scientific observations even as food supplies dwindled. Powell and his brother climbed out for the eclipse on August 7, but it rained and they could not complete their observations.

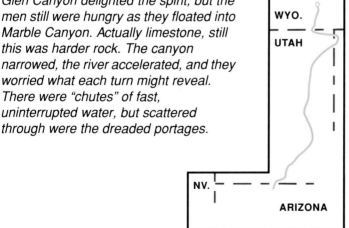

Glen Canyon delighted the spirit, but the men still were hungry as they floated into Marble Canyon. Actually limestone, still this was harder rock. The canyon narrowed, the river accelerated, and they worried what each turn might reveal. There were "chutes" of fast, uninterrupted water, but scattered through were the dreaded portages.

WYO.

UTAH

NV.

ARIZONA

Rapids with few rocks are "merely" exhilarating for modern rafts, but could roll Powell's boats like logs.

*...We find fountains bursting from the rock, high overhead, and the
spray in the sunshine forms the gems which bedeck the wall. The rocks below the
fountain are covered with mosses, and ferns, and many beautiful flowering plants....*

It was backbreaking work punctuated by beauty. The men were weary, and it was not a weariness that would pass with a night's sleep. It was in their bones, as they rowed or lifted or pushed or bailed. The *Maid of the Cañon* had a hole stove in her, and they stopped a day to make her "tight as a cup." They carried the boats. They slept in the rain. But in the midst of it there were moments of startling beauty. Once they found fountains coming from the rock, and the miracle that always happens in the desert, the bright green of water-loving plants appeared from nowhere whenever water was present.

On the last Rocky Mountain field trip, the year before, the only genuine scientist Powell had taken along was the botanist George Vasey. Sumner, and the Howland brothers, and probably Walter Powell, knew him and thought how he'd like this place, so they named it "Vasey's Paradise."

The canyon was beautiful, for the river had carved and fluted and polished the limestone walls until the men resorted to elaborate on government buildings they had seen or heard of as comparisons. Bradley said these were the most beautiful marbles he'd ever seen, "not excepting those in the Cap. at Washington." Powell wrote, "This afternoon I had a walk of a mile of a marble pavement, polished smooth in many places, in others embossed in a thousand fantastic patterns." (This is the literary Powell: certainly he knew it was limestone.) They began calling it "Marble Canyon" and we still call it that today. It is the first canyon

experience many modern boaters have at the beginning of their Grand Canyon trip.

This was August, and the afternoon storms came. When Major Powell and his brother Walter hiked out to observe the eclipse the rain foiled them, and they got caught by dark returning to camp. They tried edging their way along but in the dark and rain it became too dangerous to move about, and they had to sit out the night—"ledged up," the old timers call it.

Even the storms brought beauty with the misery. Repeatedly in Marble Canyon they saw pour-offs, as rain gathered on the slickrock above until a flood-fed stream came to the edge of the canyon and cascaded over, a temporary magnificence boatmen love. But how much can bone-weary men appreciate? Bradley's journal: "We are interested now only in how we shall get through the canon and once more to civilization."

Nankoweap Canyon, entering from the right, marked the end of Marble Canyon. From here on the journals would mention danger more than beauty.

Vasey's Paradise in Marble Canyon is on a turn, and at first appears almost a diamond-bedecked wall across the canyon. The diamonds, of course, are water—more precious in the desert than any mere jewel. They named the cascades of water and plant life for botanist George Vasey.

...We are three quarters of a mile in the depths of the earth...we are but pigmies, running up and down the sands, or lost among the boulders. We have an unknown distance yet to run; an unknown river yet to explore. What falls there are, we know not; what rocks beset the channel, we know not; what walls rise over the river, we know not....

On August 10 they came to the mouth of the Little Colorado River, coming in from the left. They had been looking for it. It was the last of the rivers that began outside the "unknown" on the map and disappeared into it, and everyone knew that somewhere in there it had to empty into the Colorado, the only river that came out. Now they had found the junction but the river was disappointing. (Visitors today sometimes have the same opinion, crossing the Little Colorado at Cameron, Arizona; but not those who see it in flood!) It was small and salty, the weather was hot, the insects uncountable. They stayed three days to make observations and accurately fix the position of the junction.

They rolled the boats over for repair, and inspected their gear and rations. The state of the gear can be guessed by the fact that Sumner carried the barometer up to measure the height of the cliff, which turned out to be 2,000 feet. Usually this was Bradley's job, but now Bradley was without shoes. That may not have been much of a problem around camp or in the boats, but imagine what that must have meant at the unavoidable portages! They sifted the lumpy, musty flour they had left through mosquito netting, boiled the worst of the bacon, and spread the dried apples to dry—again. By now they'd been soaked and re-dried repeatedly. It was not a happy camp.

The Major continued with his "geologizing," spending considerable time describing the rock layers, but Bradley's journal is more typical of what the men were thinking: "The men are uneasy and discontented and anxious to move on. If Major does not do something soon I fear the consequences, but he is contented and seems to think that biscuit made of sour and musty flour and a few dried apples is ample to sustain a laboring man. If he can only study geology he will be happy without food or shelter but the rest of us are not afflicted with it to an alarming extent."

They were ready to leave on the 13th, and as Powell and the men looked at the boats tugging at their lines in the current, they knew that if their calculations were even close to right, they were pushing off onto the final leg of the voyage. What they didn't know yet was that it would be the Grand Canyon.

The peace of views from above (here at Cape Solitude) is deceptive, as the explorers were soon to discover.

Looking back up the Colorado, the silt-laden Little Colorado enters from the right in this picture. Often when a tributary floods it brings its particular color of silt to the Colorado, making long stretches where the river is one color on one side, a different color on the other, with an abrupt line between.

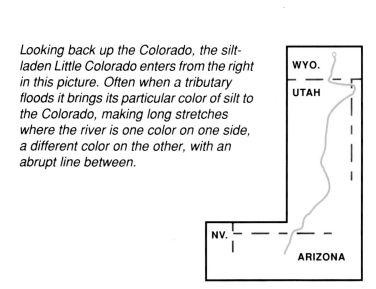

...Clouds are playing in the canyon today. Sometimes they roll down in great masses, filling the gorge with gloom; sometimes they hang above, from wall to wall, and cover the canyon with a roof of impending storm...

The walls at the mouth of the Little Colorado had been the highest they had yet seen, and the Major, high on the cliff straining to see the trend of the gorge westward, saw that the terrain got even higher. As the river had to be descending, it meant they were coming to canyons deeper than any of them had ever imagined. What would that do to the river?

They found out. An hour below camp they ran out of the red sandstone and into granite. Long ago they'd learned that hard rock meant bad rapids, and now the river carried them into the foundations of the earth, the hardest rock they'd seen. The first day into the Grand Canyon—there was no arguing about this name—they passed something like 33 rapids. They lined three of them, and this already-excruciating labor was lifted to a new level of strain. This rock did not provide shorelines for lining, so each rapid was a new challenge.

They did their old trick of stringing three boats out three lines long and catching them at the bottom. If a boat took a load of water from a reflex wave on the way through that meant snubbing more than two tons of moving mass at the bottom. Hands burned and backs strained. Night caught them halfway around a portage that was partly rock garden, partly on a ledge up the cliff. They sat huddled all night in the rain, in what rain gear they could scavenge, catching what sleep they could. Bradley mentioned the possibility of someone dropping into the river during the night but no one did. In the gray morning they all were there, looking downriver at more white water.

They encountered what they had worried about, a bad rapid that maybe you couldn't run but you certainly couldn't portage. There was simply no way around. They even tried going up a side gully onto a ledge far overhead, and walking a mile to another gully down, but it wouldn't work. So they shot through the din, drenched, one boat swamped, the others pitched to what seemed like near-vertical in some places, and made it OK.

At least on the 15th they found a good campsite, under a willow on a sandbar. While the exhausted men lay on the sand the Major explored a side canyon. They admired a clear creek that entered by their camp, even though it refused to yield fish to them. At the time they named it "Silver Creek," but the Major, on the lecture platform later, thought up "Bright Angel Creek" which is how it is known today, in the heart of Grand Canyon National Park.

In mid-August the super-heated desert can spawn spectacular afternoon thunderstorms, depicted here above Hancock Butte, Grand Canyon North Rim. Although a delight for photographers, for the exhausted men who had long ago lost their rubber ponchos it meant daily, sometimes hourly, changes from cold rain to burning sun, and back again.

WYO.

UTAH

NV.

ARIZONA

Despite a brief respite in the Grand at delightful Bright Angel Creek, the rapids, hunger, and exhaustion soon returned.

[I] discover the ruins of two or three old houses, which were originally of stone, laid in mortar....It is ever a source of wonder to us why these ancient people sought such inaccessible places for their homes....

It was time to repair boats and salvage rations again, and the camp at Bright Angel Creek was delightful. They found a pine log quite a ways up the creek, battered from being washed down from the high country where it had grown, but still preferable to the cottonwood driftwood they'd been using. They skidded it into camp and began the labor of sawing it into long strips, to be cut into oars.

Pleasant as the camp was, the rations were cause for worry. Then one of those frustrating little accidents happened: A tied boat moved unexpectedly in the eddy, sweeping its line across the rock where Billy Rhodes was making biscuits. It knocked their last baking soda into the river where it was instantly gone in the muddy water, and just as fast they were reduced to unleavened bread for the rest of the trip. The only thing they still had in good supply was coffee.

Powell explored some ruins near the canyon—familiar to many Grand Canyon National Park visitors today—and speculated again on the lives of the people who had lived in the heart of the canyon country. Hard as it was to leave the comparative comfort of this camp, it was not replenishing their supplies. They pushed off.

The expedition was losing its pretense of science and turning to survival. The barometers were out of commission, which meant they could no longer calculate the "fall" they'd come, and no longer knew now much remained before they would be out of it. Oramel Howland lost the map and notes he'd been keeping since the Little Colorado, which lessened their idea of where they were. Their goal was the Mormon settlements near where the Virgin River empties into the Colorado, after the Colorado rolls out of the Grand Canyon, somewhere west of them. But how far, and would the rations last?

If the Major's account written several years later is right, here for the first time he considered giving up the river, speculating how they could climb out and reach the Mormon settlements to the north. The weather conspired to make them miserable, chilling thunderstorms which they faced without raingear, alternating with blasting heat. They had one tarp left for shelter, hard to rig for nine men.

The *Maid of the Cañon* was damaged again; another stop for repairs. The *Emma Dean* swamped and when calmer water came the cliffs were right down to the water; they bailed her out without stopping. One wonders if they remembered the first day, way back on the Green River, when a boat took a wave they wouldn't even notice now, so they had stopped for the day and spread their bounteous supplies out to dry. Now they bailed and kept going.

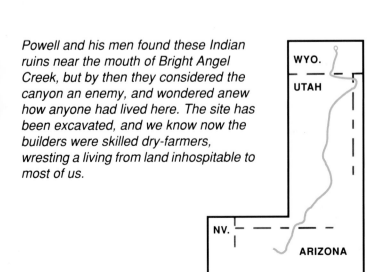

Powell and his men found these Indian ruins near the mouth of Bright Angel Creek, but by then they considered the canyon an enemy, and wondered anew how anyone had lived here. The site has been excavated, and we know now the builders were skilled dry-farmers, wresting a living from land inhospitable to most of us.

WYO.

UTAH

NV.

ARIZONA

The expedition called this Silver Creek. Later Powell changed it to Bright Angel Creek, he said to balance the Dirty Devil.

Our rations are still spoiling; the bacon is so badly injured that we are compelled to throw it away....We have now only musty flour sufficient for ten days, a few dried apples, but plenty of coffee....

Below Bright Angel Creek there are a series of side canyons. Each of these spews boulders into the Colorado when in flood, so the mouth of each side canyon is marked with a rapid in the Colorado. It is indicative of the mood of the men that repeatedly the next rapid was "the worst we've seen," or "the wildest yet."

The Colorado was rising and muddy. They were riding on floodwaters from any number of the dozens of side canyons they'd passed in three months. This was the drain of the Rocky Mountains, and runoff from remote valleys in the Rockies, from the San Juans, water from the northwestern plains of New Mexico, from the drainage of the Green in Wyoming, all bore them now. The mud, in fact, was the very stuff of the Rockies, ground fine and being carried to the ocean, tiny victories in erosion's constant struggle with uplift.

The rains continued, sometimes all night and at morning, breaking the usual pattern of afternoon thundershowers. One morning was sunny and Powell decided they could stay in camp to dry their bedding, but the next morning dawned gray and rainy again. The bacon was too far gone so they threw it away. There was nothing to supplement their pitiful supplies, and it seems certain they were suffering the effects of starvation by now. One evening Bradley threatened "all sorts of revenge when I get to decent food once more."

Powell was concerned too, but the geology was irresistible. It's understandable; imagine being the first geologist to visit the Grand Canyon. He climbed until the river was a silent brook far below, and still as much canyon remained above him as below. Of that hike he wrote, "All about me are interesting geologic records. The book is open and I can read as I run."

They emerged from the granite, but occasionally the dark rock would arise about them again, then descend. Discouragingly, the course of the river turned almost east again. This not only meant they were going away from Callville; it meant they might reenter the granite. Would this place ever end?

A quarter-continent's water was gathered in the Grand, from snowpack in the Rockies to springs and trickles up unknown canyons, at times creating ephemeral waterfalls like this one.

Near the end the journals seem almost a blur of effort and agony. Rapids such as Granite are dangerous today even with superb equipment and boatmen who have run it repeatedly; then they were clearly impossible. So shoeless men, weakened by borderline starvation, once more manhandled their deteriorating boats around however they could.

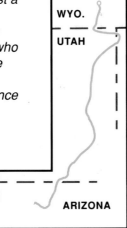

WYO.

UTAH

NV.

ARIZONA

...I stand on deck, supporting myself with a strap, fastened on either side to the gunwale, and the boat glides rapidly where the water is smooth, or, striking a wave, she leaps and bounds like a thing of life, and we have a wild, exhilarating ride for ten miles....

The river's turn back to the east concerned the exhausted crew, and Bradley feared arriving back where they'd come from, fooled like "the old hog when he moved the hollow log so that both ends came on the outside of the fence." But on August 21 the river turned west again. Good news. Every mile that direction was a mile closer to the end.

Some of those miles moved by quickly. Powell's quote above describes the exhilaration of the ride in a chute, where there can be a surge of current without the danger of rocks. Of course one could not be sure, and this particular incident happened when the current had not allowed them to stop when they'd wanted to and they swept around a blind bend toward unscouted rapids. More often, of course, the rocks forced caution or the hated labor of lining or even skidding the boats.

Sometimes being on the river was not the worst part of the 24 hours: "So we gather driftwood and build a fire; but after supper [unleavened bread] the rain, coming down in torrents, extinguishes it, and we sit up all night on the rocks, shivering, and are more exhausted by the night's discomfort than by the day's toil."

Only half the men had shoes, all the ponchos they'd packed at Green River were gone, more than half the men did not have hats, and there weren't enough blankets to go around. Not only was their personal gear wearing out, but the boats needed re-

caulking every day now, and constant repairs. Beside the danger, a leaky boat was heavy and hard to handle or row. They were wet almost all of the time anyway now, but a leaky boat guaranteed it. Tough skin softened in the water, and constantly wet clothes made sitting in one place on the boat's board seat almost unbearable. Sunburn aggravated abrasions and scrapes. Occasionally the phrase "felt unwell" shows up in their journals, and the only surprise is that it isn't more often.

Six out of seven nights it rained, so the men were relieved when they came to a huge alcove and the Major called an early camp. Assured of shelter from the rain, they built a roaring bonfire and had the first good night's sleep in a week. To boot, the next day they thought the canyon was wider. Could they be near the end?

After the toil of a rapid like Tapeats, bed was where you found it, sometimes a boulder field.

From upstream, rapids can appear deceptively easy, but the view from below shows what the men faced. To the picture must be added the thunderous noise, drowning the voices of men yelling advice or caution, rushing afloat or thrashing barefoot over the rocks at the torrent's edge, manhandling the boats.

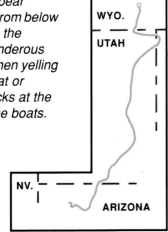

WYO.

UTAH

NV.

ARIZONA

...We come to monuments of lava...

It's easy for starving, exhausted men to personalize a canyon as a foe, and this one seemed to be playing with them. Information they had begun with about supposed forays into the canyon from the lower end had told them it was 70 miles from the mouth of the Little Colorado to Grand Wash, a known tributary to the Colorado they would come to after they left the Grand Canyon, with an easy run from there to the Virgin River. They now knew that was fantasy—they'd come over 120 miles since the Little Colorado already, and the rapids seemed to be getting worse even as men and boats were wearing out. The iron strap, bent into a loop, which the bow line of one boat was tied to pulled out at a critical moment. Quick work avoided disaster when they got a line snubbed onto the stern of the boat before it was out of control, but it was a close thing.

At another "worst rapid yet," today's Lava Falls, Powell found a new and unexpected bit of geology, which he had no problem working out. They began to discover great lava blocks in and along the river, and at a place where a fault crosses the canyon came upon a virtual waterfall. The scene was clear, when you put the clues together. Far up on the rim they could see a cinder cone (which they had spotted on a climb some days before), and one could still see where the lava had flowed into the already-existing canyon, and may have dammed it to a height of 1,500 feet. But the river had managed to cut through the blockage, at least down to the level of the falls that was left.

Molten lava meeting the Colorado River—what a battle of Titans! When the flow ceased and hardened it dammed the river. Still the tremendous waterfall that must have come over the dam gradually wore it down, to the rapid Powell's men portaged.

K.C. DEN DOOVEN

Sometimes the geologic "book of earth's history" reads like high drama. Far up on the rim is "Vulcan's Throne," a volcanic cinder cone. Near it lava emerged and flowed into the canyon, an unstoppable, incandescent molten rockfall. The columnar jointing was formed in the cooling process. Today, ocotillo plants make the scene peaceful.

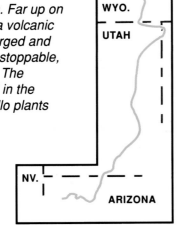

They dragged the heavy boats out of the water and around the falls; at least the lack of supplies meant there was that much less to carry. Re-launched, they floated peacefully and Powell took the chance to reason out what had happened from the patches of lava that still clung to the canyon walls. He could see the scene, and undoubtedly explained it to the men.

In his account he gives it exclamation points: "What a conflict of water and fire there must have been here! Just imagine a river of molten rock running down into a river of melted snow. What a seething and boiling of the waters; what clouds of steam rolled into the heavens!" Then followed the more serious and immediate, also deserving the exclamation mark: "Thirty-five miles to-day. Hurrah!"

...All night long, I pace up and down a little path, on a few yards of sand beach, along by the river. Is it wise to go on?...But for years I have been contemplating this trip. To leave the exploration unfinished, to say that there is a part of the canyon which I cannot explore....I determine to go on.

It was true they were cascading toward the end now, but the few days remaining would discover a few more tricks of the river, and one would be fatal. They wasted no daylight hours, but rowed or carried or floated until dark forced them to quit. On August 25th they had opened the last bag of flour. On the 26th the river seemed to open up a little and they made 35 miles with only one portage. And, wonder of wonder, they found food. They came across an Indian farm with nobody home, and took squash, "excusing ourselves by pleading our great want." They floated downstream until they thought no Indian could follow, then stopped and cooked up the squash. With unleavened bread and coffee it was a feast.

They came to the climax of the trip on the 27th, and at first it was just another bad rapid. But this one was not just bad, it was unrunnable, or at least so it seemed to their weakened spirits and bodies. "Separation Rapid" had such billows that they thought they would be lost even if they could avoid the rocks, but doubted they could do even that. The lay of the canyon made it impossible to scout the rapid adequately, and no matter how they climbed, they could find no way around it. Bradley summed it up: "The spectacle is appalling to us." They camped, worried.

After supper Oramel Howland asked to talk with Powell, and they walked along the river. Howland told Powell that he and his brother, Seneca, and William Dunn, would go no further. They had decided to hike out, and suggested that the whole expedition

ought to do so. They would drown in this rapid; three more bad ones were in sight below it, and they were out of rations. They had decided their best chance was to work their way out a side canyon and try to get to the Mormon settlements. Powell argued, but Howland said the trio had made up their minds.

All night long Powell paced on the little sand bar, judging options. What if they were right? It was important to get the data the expedition had gathered back, or the whole thing was a waste. Still, judging the uncertainty of finding a way out, the distance to the settlements, and the work of the boats so far, he decided it was best go to on.

Probably few slept that night, the muffled rumble of the unscouted rapid a backdrop to Powell's pacing. In the morning the group was somber, each faction thinking the other had made the wrong decision. The hikers were offered part of the remaining rations, but refused, confident they could shoot game enroute. They took two rifles and a shotgun, and duplicate notes of the journey in case they were the ones who made it back to civilization and the boatmen perished. When all was said that could be, the hikers watched the boatmen push off and disappear around the bend toward the unrunnable rapid.

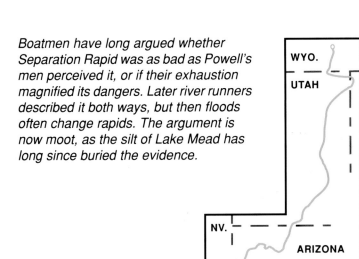

Boatmen have long argued whether Separation Rapid was as bad as Powell's men perceived it, or if their exhaustion magnified its dangers. Later river runners described it both ways, but then floods often change rapids. The argument is now moot, as the silt of Lake Mead has long since buried the evidence.

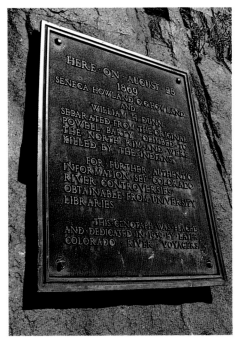

Another controversy starts here: Were the men who left "deserters"? Powell never described them as such, nor did the journals written at the time. The question arose later.

...Now the danger is over; now the toil has ceased; now the gloom has disappeared...The river rolls by us in silent majesty; the quiet of the camp is sweet; our joy is almost ecstasy. We sit till long after midnight, talking of the Grand Canyon, talking of home....

They were not out of it. This rapid was a roarer and the day brought eleven more, including one that nearly killed Bradley and actually panicked Powell.

With the reduced crew they'd decided to leave behind the *Emma Dean,* which was slowly disintegrating anyway. So in the two oak boats, nerves tight, they rowed for the lip where the water surged out of sight and were committed. It was a wild ride. They filled with water right away, which might actually have helped as they plunged through the tailwaves. But both boats made it. Bailing in an eddy, they fired guns in case Dunn and the Howland brothers would decide to take the *Emma Dean* and follow them, but no one appeared.

The rapid that nearly ended the expedition came in mid-afternoon. It had to be lined, and the men slowly let the *Maid of the Cañon* down by rope, Bradley in her using an oar to keep her off the rocks. The boat reached the very lip of the fall where the current was strongest...and they ran out of rope. Unable to pull back against the current and fearing to let go, they snubbed the rope to a rock while two men ran back to the *Kitty Clyde's Sister* for another rope.

Powell, up on the cliff, saw the heavy boat at the end of the line begin to swing out and then back toward the cliff with crushing force. Bradley, in extreme danger, frantically fended the boat off the cliff with an oar. Choosing to run the rapid willy-nilly rather than shattering the boat, he pulled his knife to cut the line but before he could the entire sternpost pulled out and shot thirty feet in the air as the damaged boat went cascading over the rapids.

Mostly it was luck, but Bradley used the one oar as best he could and came through the maelstrom soaked, exhilarated, heart pounding, and waving his hat to show the upstream watchers he was OK. But for the only time on the trip, it appears the Major had panicked. Shouting at Hawkins and Hall to scramble along the cliff to help, he and Sumner tumbled into the *Kitty Clyde's Sister* and shoved off for the same rapid. They filled, then rolled, and the Major wrote he had no idea what happened until Bradley, whom they were rushing to save, pulled them out of the water. All through, shaken but safe.

It sounds like a novel, but it was their last rapid. The next day, August 29, was the red-letter day of the trip. The dreaded black granite sank back into the earth, and before noon the canyon walls came back to river level. They floated out of the Grand Canyon into rolling country. The Powell quote above is from that night. They sat by the fires, success (and something to eat) assured within days, and talked of rapids, canyons, and campsites known only to them, of all the people on the globe that night. They talked of their companions, even then making their way out—maybe. It was a good night.

Shortly after noon the next day they came upon four men seining fish at the mouth of the Virgin River. It turned out they were also watching for debris floating down the river, of the long-given-up John Wesley Powell Expedition to explore the Colorado River.

Joshua trees, where the Colorado becomes a slow, flatland river.

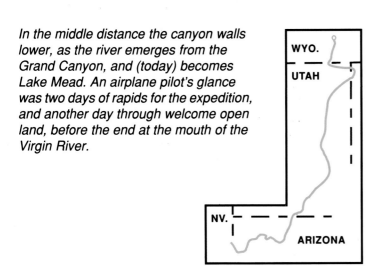

In the middle distance the canyon walls lower, as the river emerges from the Grand Canyon, and (today) becomes Lake Mead. An airplane pilot's glance was two days of rapids for the expedition, and another day through welcome open land, before the end at the mouth of the Virgin River.

WYO.

UTAH

NV.

ARIZONA

The Colorado River at today's river mile 148.

They had lived with intensity. On the lip of a rapid, every nerve is a bowstring, and details freeze like frames in a film. Battered like a ball they'd bounced between peace and danger, fear and fun, life and even death. Yet behind it, for Powell, was an ever grander adventure: to know what was here, how it had come to be, and how the Americans even then spilling westward would live in the arid land. But the river itself had stolen back his data. By the Grand Canyon they'd lost most of it in swampings, with even the instruments needed to gain more. So he came back. In 1871-72 Powell directed another expedition, with all new members. They ran the river in sections, resupplied, and spent months triangulating and measuring the plateaus and canyons. An adventurer-schoolteacher had emerged as a serious scientist, and the country was the richer.

Powell's Men

John Colton Sumner (1840-1907)

Civil War veteran turned mountain man. Fought in the 32nd Iowa Volunteer Infantry. After the war he became a trading post operator and outfitter in Middle Park, Colorado. Powell recognized his skills during the Rocky Mountain Exploring Expeditions and hired him for the boat trip. Brother-in-law to W. N. Byers, influential editor of the *Rocky Mountain News*, Sumner worked for Powell again in later surveys, but became embittered and as an old man was the source of many anti-Powell stories.

George Young Bradley (1836-1885)

Served in the Civil War with the 19th Massachusetts Volunteer Infantry, wounded at Fredericksburg. Reenlisted after the war and served at various frontier forts. Powell met him at Fort Bridger in 1869 and arranged a discharge so he could go on the trip. Kept the best journal of the trip.

Walter Henry Powell (1842-1915)

The Major's younger brother. He served in the 2nd Illinois Artillery, becoming a captain. He was captured in sight of John Wesley at Atlanta in 1864, and apparently had a breakdown while in a Confederate prison, from which he never fully recovered. Worked hard on the trip, moody, extremely strong, and occasionally broke into song.

William Rhodes Hawkins (1841-1919)

"Billy" Rhodes, who later added the Hawkins, apparently after some brush with the law. Served in the 9th Regiment, Missouri Cavalry. Not much is known of him. He served competently on the expedition.

Oramel G. Howland (1833-1869)

Vermonter. Apparently well educated, became printer and editor in Denver on the *Rocky Mountain News*. Spent much time in the wilderness, and worked (with Sumner) as guide on Powell's earlier expeditions, then signed on for the river trip. Killed after departing the expedition at Separation Rapid.

Seneca B. Howland (1843-1869)

Younger brother of Oramel. Served in the Civil War with the 16th Vermont Infantry, and was wounded at Gettysburg. Killed with brother and Dunn, after climbing out at Separation Rapid.

William Dunn (d. 1869)

Little is known of Dunn prior to his appearance at Middle Park in 1868 to work for Powell, other than the latter's statement that Dunn had been a trapper for years. He was one of the trio who died climbing out at Separation Rapid. Apparently worked quietly and well on the trip.

Andrew Hall (1851-1882)

Young "Andy" already had considerable frontier experience at the age of 18 when Powell met him at the put-in, and hired him. Good choice; he was young, green, enthusiastic, cheery. After the expedition ended at the Virgin River, he and Billy Rhodes took a boat on down the Colorado, just to do it.

Frank Goodman

Goodman was the English adventurer who appeared at Green River and joined the expedition, lost all his gear in the wreck of the *No Name*, and left the expedition at the Uinta River. Nothing else is known of him.

Born March 24, 1834, John Wesley Powell had a keen interest in science even as a youngster, and became a schoolteacher at age 16 to earn money for a college education. Severely wounded at Shiloh during the Civil War, Powell's right arm had to be amputated just below the elbow, but this misfortune didn't dim his eagerness to use his scientific knowledge and explore the unknown. His wife, Emma Dean, shared his enthusiasm and accompanied him on two trips into the Colorado Rocky Mountains. After seeing the headwaters of the Grand, the Major began preparations for his first, and most famous, expedition down the Colorado in 1869. He obtained government support for a second Colorado River expedition in 1871-72, and the success of his findings led later to his dual appointments as director of the Bureau of Ethnology (1879) and the Geological Survey (1881). Following his resignation due to failing health in 1894, honors continued to come his way until his peaceful death at their summer home in Maine on September 23, 1902.

*...The clouds are children
of the heavens, and when they
play among the rocks they lift them
to the region above....*

August 15, 1869.

Epilogue

The expedition returned from the dead, as the public viewed it, as something approaching national heros. Nor would the drama stop. Word came that three white men had been killed by Shivwits Indians, and Powell went back to learn that it was indeed Dunn and the Howland brothers. The three had managed to climb out of the canyon all right, but then were killed by Indians who mistook them for some miners who had recently committed outrages on the Indians. It is remarkable, but Powell was able to accept this, and cemented a relationship with the Shivwits which allowed his men to work among them in future years with relative safety.

Powell was no mere adventurer. If that were true, the first trip would have been enough. But he returned in 1871-72, this time better prepared (though he still didn't catch on to the flaws in his boat design—they went in cigars again), and with supplies packed to the river at certain points, now that they had a rough idea of the routes. Every loss in adventure was a gain in data returned, the reason for the expedition.

Seizing the moment of the public's immense curiosity about the adventure on the unknown river, Powell wrote *The Exploration of the Colorado River and its Canyons,* first for magazines and then as a book, which was an immediate best seller. The adventure had caught the public's mind. Now comes a puzzle of Powell's life, which remains unsolved. When he became a writer, Powell, the man who insisted on *measuring* the river and the land, and even went back the second time to get the data right, wrote an eloquent account in which he simply combined the two voyages into one.

He mentioned only the crew of the first trip, but casually mixed events from both trips into one great adventure, possibly elaborating a few extra for good measure. Most of it can be sorted out by journals and scraps of information from other men on the trips, but that Powell did it remains a mystery. Furthermore, the rest of his career was conducted with rigid scientific standards. It simply doesn't fit, and probably says something of the complexity of the man.

Irony: The fame and influence that followed the book was the engine that drove Powell's career in its early stages, a career devoted to data-based, scientific ends. He helped organize the United States Geological Survey and became its second director. It was a new breed of government agency, devoted not to the political ends of the party in power, but to independent study of the brute facts. How much rain falls? Where are the resources? The idea was to discover and present the facts, so the politicians and the people would at least have something solid to build their dreams on.

Setting the course for the USGS, he began the immense job of creating high-standard maps of the entire United States, including the topographicals familiar to hikers today. A century after Powell scrambled up and down the cliffs with his clumsy barometer, measuring the thickness of the strata, a regiment of geologists of the USGS is out there on any good day or even rainy ones, poking around, mapping, measuring, reporting.

Not content to put bureaucratic feet on geology, Powell also began the Bureau of American Ethnography within the Smithsonian, and was its first director. Soon Washington presses began to roll off the thick annual BAE "Reports," thumbed daily by anthropology students in university libraries all over the world.

Let us grant to the pedantic that the great contribution of Powell to the country was his later bureaucratic career. He seemed to relish the political maneuvering, and gained remarkable skill at it (perhaps remembering back to '68, when he'd come in as an audacious green school teacher from the plains of Illinois, vainly looking for backing for his splendid field trip down the Colorado), but behind the maneuvering he had a clear vision that has proven itself to the national good a hundredfold: the need for data before the dreaming.

Still, one wonders if the bureaucratic wars in forcing a marriage between government and science is what he dreamed of, when he was an old man in his apartment in Washington, D.C., or the summer home in Maine where he died? One time he had camped on sandbars in the rain, and scrambled up cliff walls to be astonished at a wonderland of geological "hoodoos" stretching everywhere. He had clung one-armed to a pitching wooden boat in the din of a monstrous rapid and screamed at his men, "Pull, Men, Pull for your lives!"—and meant it.

Almost unbelievably for a life so close to our own, before middle age he had run unknown canyons, discovered and named rivers and mountain ranges, and learned to know as few outsiders did the culture of the people who lived there. And one day, a hot summer day 'way back in 1869, he'd come floating out of the Grand Canyon and seen men fishing on the bank, and waiting for him. *Now that was a moment!*

Books in the Voyage of Discovery series: Lewis & Clark, Oregon Trail, John Wesley Powell

Published by KC Publications • Creators of The Story Behind the Scenery
Box 14429 • Las Vegas, NV 89114

Printed by Dong-A Printing and Publishing, Seoul, Korea
Color Separations by Kedia/Kwangyangsa Co., Ltd.